Also by Jerry Van Amerongen

Minnows in the Bath
and Other
Doggie Treats

by Jerry Van Amerongen

Andrews McMeel
Publishing

Kansas City

For Tillie

00 01 02 03 04 BAH 10 9 8 7 6 5 4 3 2 1

ISBN: 0-7407-0579-2

Library of Congress Catalog Card Number: 99-68671

Introduction

I have often been asked if I own a dog, and if he or she gives me ideas for my dog cartoons. My dog's name is Tillie. Miss Tillie we call her. She is a yellow Lab with just a hint of Chesapeake Bay retriever. She'll be fifteen years old next month. Miss Tillie is quite trim and very refined. She moves about the house with great care and grace. I suppose it's a lot like living with a sixty-pound cat.

Tillie often gives me an entry point into an idea, but then it's usually filtered through some other dog's personality or circumstance. One idea, however, that's directly attributable to Tillie, or I should say to my wife, Linda, is a little something we do when we return home from an evening out. Over the years Linda has managed to talk me into kneeling with her on the floor next to Tillie. We then lay our hands on Miss Tillie and begin chanting, "healing hands! healing hands!" We do this over and over. My wife thinks this might take the sting out of being left home alone. I think it helps explain the knotted brow and troubled look on Miss Tillie's face.

Tillie is not without her quirks. Our neighbor Jane, who often takes care of Tillie when we travel, has said, "Having Miss Tillie in the house is like having an eccentric aunt come to visit."

She's been our companion for a very long time. She spends her days lounging in a soft doggie bed next to my drawing board, but she's as alert as ever and lobbies hard when the time comes for one of her many daily walks to the woods at the end of our street.

When she was younger, she covered a lot of ground quickly, sniffing indiscriminately, always looking ahead. Now, at fifteen years, she covers far less ground, quietly, sniffing leisurely, taking in much more of the world she traverses. Dogs can teach us a lot about growing old.

—Jerry Van Amerongen
December 1999

Miss tillie takes a nap.

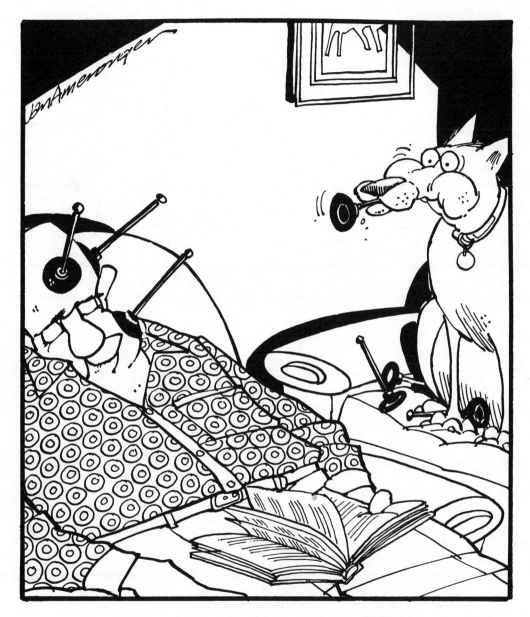

So! Those worrisome facial blotches of Ken's
do have something to do with his napping.

Ben wonders if it's not too late to restructure
his relationship with his dog, Baxter.

"Hi, folks! Buster just wants to say hi!"

Well, that's it for reading!

Buck's owner is an air-flow consultant.

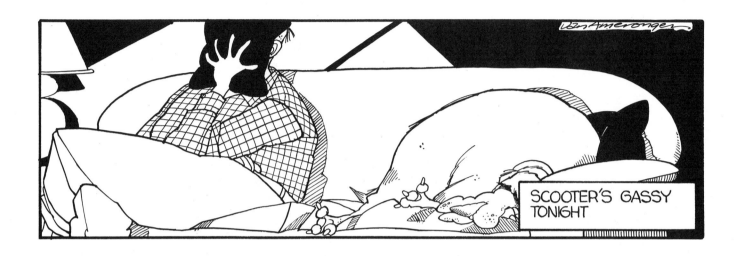

It's a slippery slope indeed, once you start trying to
prove to your pet how yummy his food tastes.

Sometimes, Russell likes to stand above his dog
and pretend he's tipping over.

Gordon could use more friends.

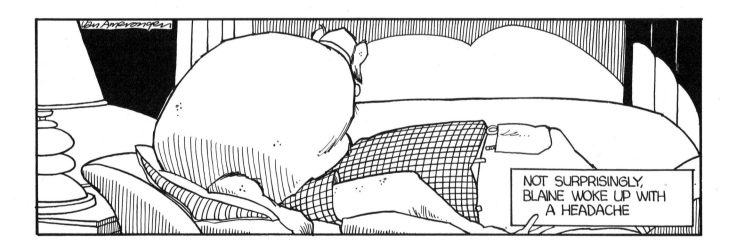

"Do we enjoy a good dog trick, Mr. Dexter?"

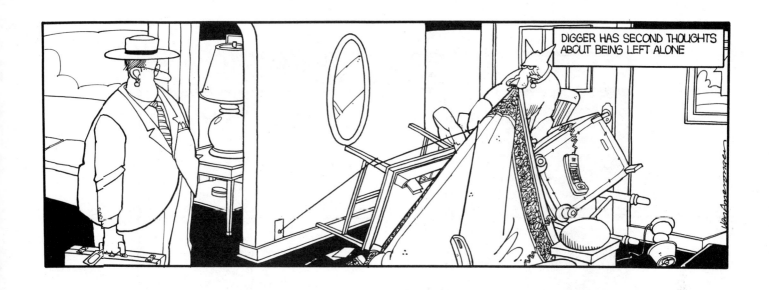

The plan is hatched for Scooter's seat.

"He's doing it again, Harold!"

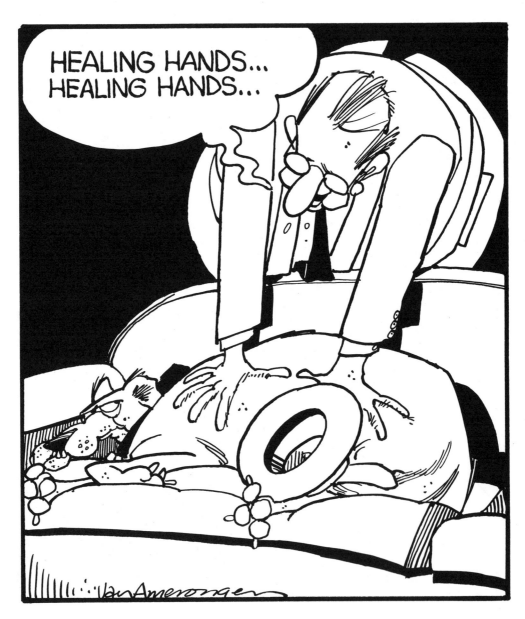

Blaine makes amends for being gone all day.

Buster delivers a negative critique of another motorist.

"Oh, look everyone! . . . page 17, column 5,
a nice piece on Medieval pottery!"

"Hold your horses!"

The new Sparky gets the willies when
he really starts thinking about the old Sparky.

. . . Which is precisely why Mr. Gordon prefers a homemade pet.

If you can't find the ribs, chances are your pet is overweight.

"OK, OK, you don't have to smile!"

Little Pancho has yet to come to terms with Bob's alone time.

Along about midweek, the Swensens like to shake things up.

NOBODY WAS SORRIER TO SEE THE OLD OAK GO THAN SCOOTER

BUSTER EATS LIKE A KING

WITH ROGER, IT'S ALL A BIT TIRESOME AFTER AWHILE

THE SWIMMERS HELPER

"NOW, REMEMBER! YOU CAN'T SWIM, BUT YOU MUST GET TO THE OTHER SIDE!"

"A cheeseburger, and hurry!"

"Ah, we appear to have selected a perfectly acceptable Cabernet!"

"We weren't very good, were we, Woodrow ..."

At home with correctional professional Lyle Burkes.

What bothers Russell is knowing the neighbor's dog is over there trying to catch his scent, as if he were common trash.

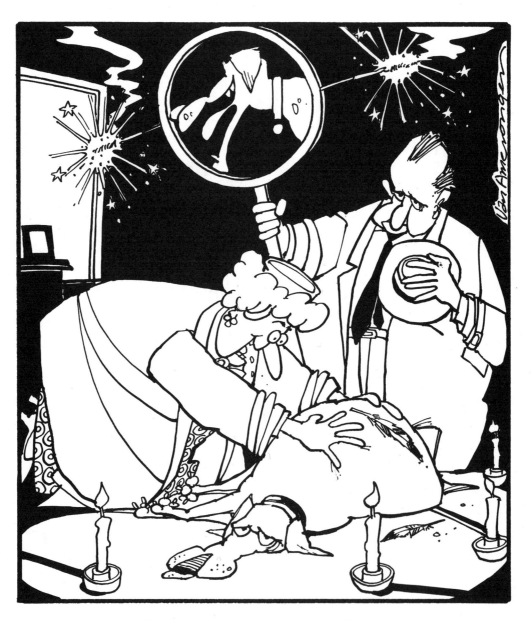

Might they be going too far with the
welcome home ceremony? , . . . Ted wonders.

"I've lost all feeling in my right foot!"

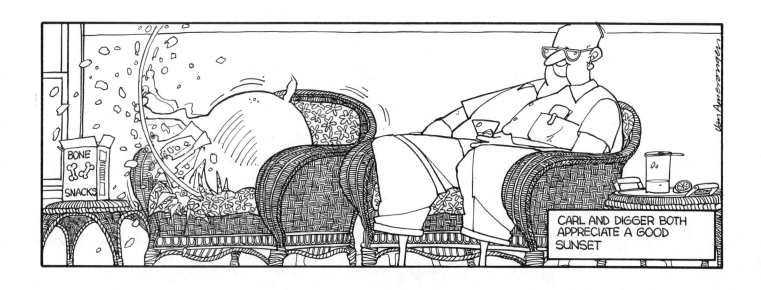

Vague genetic impulses cause Digger to feel a sense of shame
at his inability to bury, thus protect, his own food.

Susie engages in a sudden burst of post-menopausal zest.

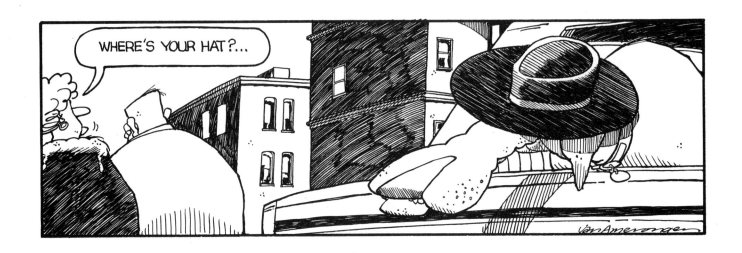

Garrett was in the Signal Corps.

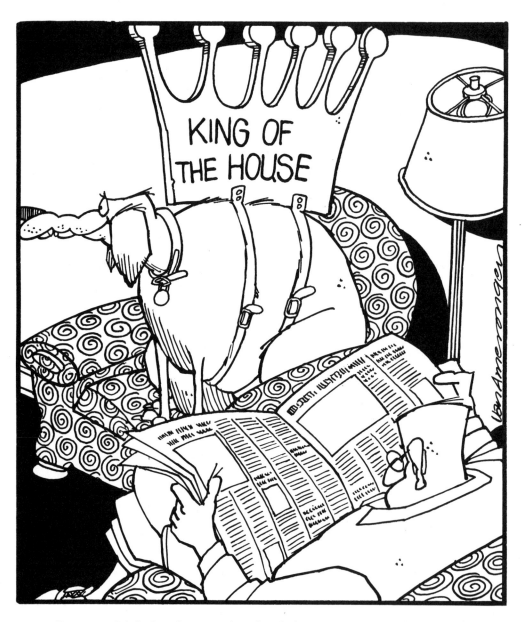

Guess which family member had the most exemplary day?

"Perhaps if I were to explain the policy options to your owner?!"

Mr. Howard's been this way before.

Rusty's life took a dark turn when Nathan bought
"The Big Book of Fishermen's Knots."

Connie and Blaine have done their part to
muffle Scooter's natural browsing instincts.

Dan and Rusty watch squirrel slides.

94

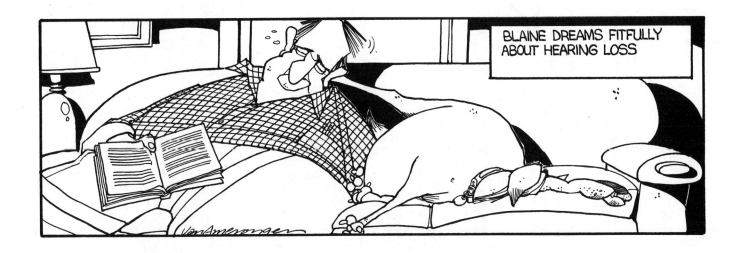

"Yes, Sparky, what is it?!"

The evening's activities wind down
over at Scooter and Blaine's house.

"Would this be an area of behavior we should
be taking a look at, Mrs. Courtney?"

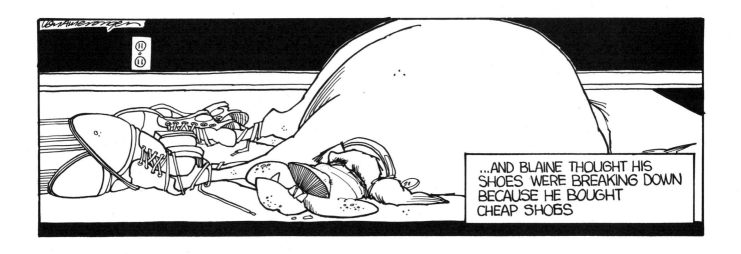

...AND BLAINE THOUGHT HIS SHOES WERE BREAKING DOWN BECAUSE HE BOUGHT CHEAP SHOES

I ASKED HIM TWO OR THREE TIMES IF HE HAD TO GO OUT!

BUT SEE, THAT PROBABLY GOT HIM THINKING ABOUT IT...

Another tedious evening over at Bowser's house.

It was the first dog Spot saw all day that
he thought he had a chance to bully.

Evidently, Beatrice has won some sort of prize.

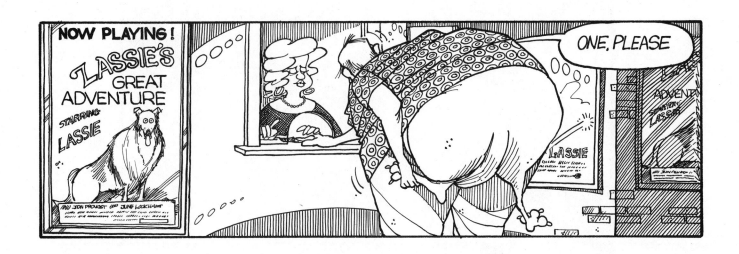

One of those special moments as Scooter is
favorably drawn to his reflection.

. . . Thus providing Spot with a quick, efficient territorial overview.

The last anyone saw, Little Rosco was fooling around by the bike on the hill in front of the cottage.

A kind of gloom settles over Scooter as his
"king of the doggies" weekend draws to a close.

"No treats for you young man, and I think you know why!"

Another overwhelmingly urbanized pet.

Watching Mr. Belding heading for work, it's not surprising
he owns his own company.

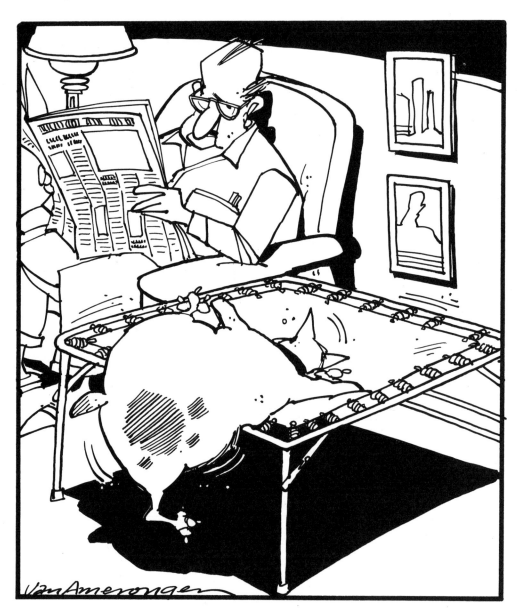

"Not tonight, Baxter."

"Arnold, where are you going with Muffin?"

The Drexler's wonder why Scooter can't
mark his territory like other dogs.

Often times Leon will dress Striker as one of our past presidents.

. . . And of course he always does.

It's going all wrong for pet guru, Russell "Moon Wind" Chambers.

Bill gives unto Socks the always appreciated
"double ear scrooggels."

Buster moves about in fits and starts.

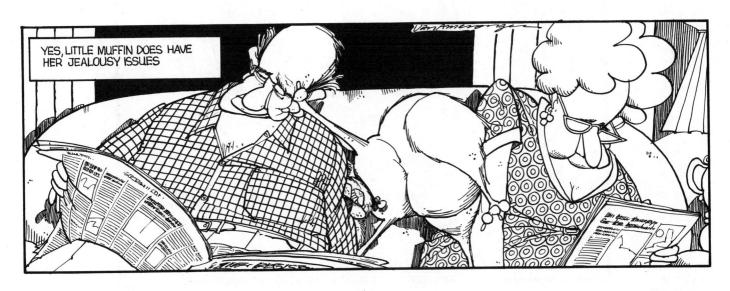

It's a helpful aid thought-up by Mrs. Nimmers
for her older dog, Susie.